# CFA 2026 LEVEL 1: ECONOMICS

## Complete in just 1-week

Dr. M. Imran Ahsan Dhothar

Cover design by: Art Painter
Library of Congress Control Number: 2018675309
Printed in the United States of America

*To all smart learners*

# CONTENTS

# LEARNING MODULE 1:

**FIRMs AND MARKET STRUCTURES**

1: Determine and interpret breakeven and shutdown points of production, as well as how economies and diseconomies of scale affect cost under perfect and imperfect competition.

**Short run time period**: This is the time in which at least one factor of production, for example, capital, is fixed. We can only increase our production by increasing units of labor, as labor can be changed easily in comparison to capital.

**Long run time period:** It is the time. In which all factors of production are variable, a firm can change its production by increasing units of capital and units of labor.

All costs are variable in this time. For example, a firm can increase its production by installing new plant and machinery, hiring new workers, or it can reduce its cost by cutting down the plant and machinery.

**Fixed cost:** It is the cost that does not change as the production level changes. This is true up to some extent, for example, the rent of a factory building. The owner of the factory has to pay a fixed amount of rent regardless of whether he produces 1 unit or 100 units.

**Variable cost:** It is the cost that changes with the change in production level. For example, the cost of raw material. When we produce more units of shoes, we need more leather, so the cost of leather increases (so it is a variable cost).

Total cost = variable cost + fixed cost

Average cost = Total cost/output

Average variable cost = variable cost/output

Average fixed cost = Fixed cost/output

We can discuss shutdown and break-even points under two conditions.;

1. Shutdown and break-even point under perfect competition.

2. Shut down and break-even point under imperfect competition.

**Perfect competition** is the situation in the market in which there is a very large number of buyers and sellers and no one can affect the prevailing prices individually.

**Imperfect competition:** It is the market situation in which characteristics of perfect competition are not fulfilled. In this type of market structure, there are many buyers but fewer sellers than buyers. Depending on the degree of competition, sellers have control over prices. Imperfect market structures include monopoly (with a single seller), monopolistic competition (with many sellers), etc.

In the coming LOS, we will discuss these structures in detail.


Total revenues are price times quantity sold. TR = PxQ.

Average revenues = TR/Q

Marginal revenues = change in TR by producing one extra output.

**Shutdown and break-even point under perfect competition**

Under perfect competition Average revenues = TR/Q = P =AR =MR

In the short run, if a firm is able to cover its variable costs, it should operate to minimize costs. It means the price is just enough to cover variable costs. If price is below the average variable cost, then the firm should shut down temporarily (in the short run).

In the long run, if the price is less than its average total cost, it should shut it down.

**Break even and shout down points by using the marginal revenue and marginal cost approach**

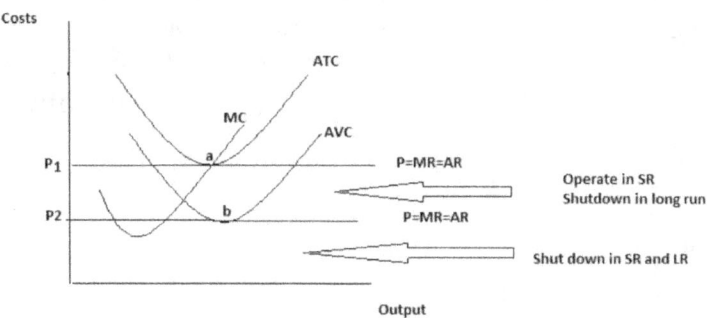

At point "a" the price P1 is just covering all costs so it is the breakeven point. At this point and above the firm should operate in short run and in long run. In the area below point "a" the firm should operate in SR as it is at least covering its variable cost. Below point "b" the firm should shut down its operations as it cannot cover both variable and total cost.

We can deduce following points from above discussion.

In short run:

If P=>ATC it's the breakeven

AVC<=P<=ATC firm should operate

P<AVC shut down

*In long run:*

If P=>ATC it's the breakeven

AVC<=P<=ATC shut down

P<AVC shut down

<= means less than or equal to.

## Shutdown and break-even point under imperfect competition

The break even and shutdown points can be explained in imperfect competition using MR and MC approach. Remember here we do not have MR =P. We have different curves of MR and AR which are downward sloping (not straight line as in perfect competition).

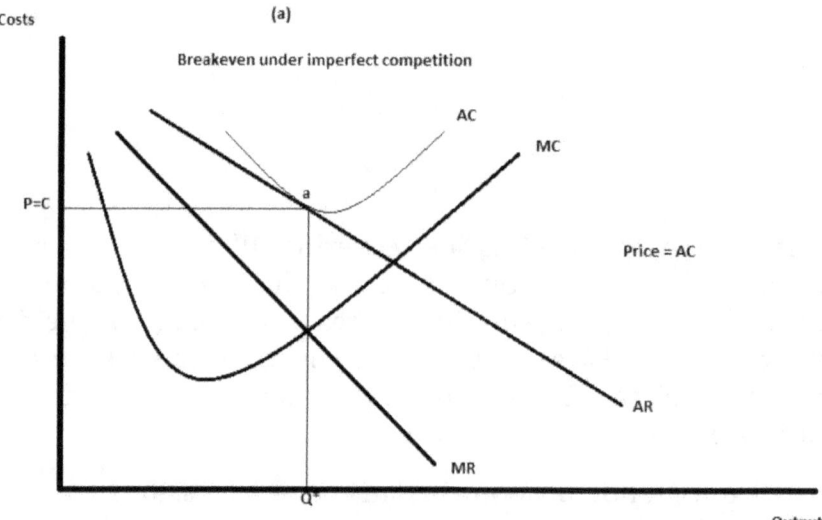

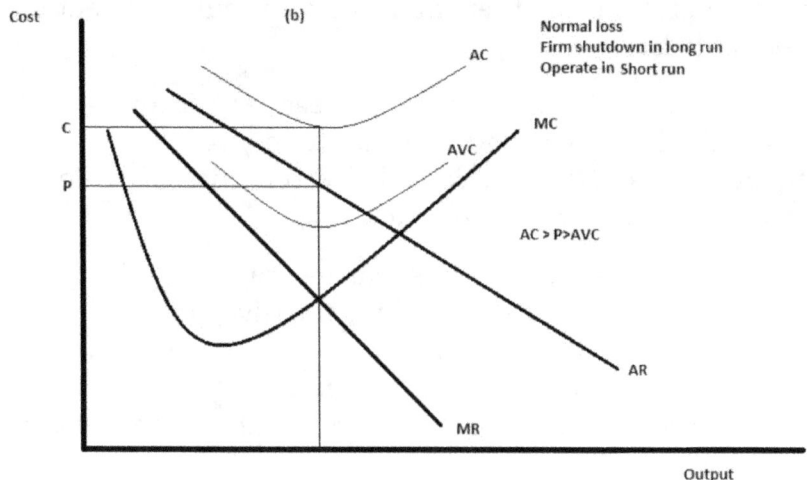

As shown in the above figure at point "a" price is equal to AC. At this point the firm is at break even.

If the firm is at break-even, the firm should operate in the short run and in the long run.

If the firm is in (b) figure`s position, it should run in the short run but should shut down in the long run as the price does not cover the total average cost, but the variable cost is being fulfilled.

If even variable cost was not being covered, then the firm should shut down in both the short and long run.

## How economies of scale and diseconomies of scale affect costs

We know that the average total cost is U-shaped. The long-run average total cost curve (LRATC) is made up of joining the minimum points of the short-run average total cost curves. LRATC shows a larger scale of production. The minimum point of LRATC is known as the minimum efficient scale. The firm should operate at this minimum efficient scale in the long run.

In perfect competition, the price is equal to the minimum cost, and the firm earns zero economic profit (also known as normal profit). Production level other than this minimum efficient scale will produce losses.

This LRATC curve decreases at first, reaches its lowest point, and eventually increases from that lowest point. The decreasing portion of the LRATC curve is called economies of scale (also known as increasing returns to scale).

LRATC decreases due to the factors that are only applicable in large production, like labor specialization, massive production, use of more efficient equipment, the most sophisticated machinery and plant, and also discounts in raw material purchases. This reduction in cost makes the firm more competitive in the market.

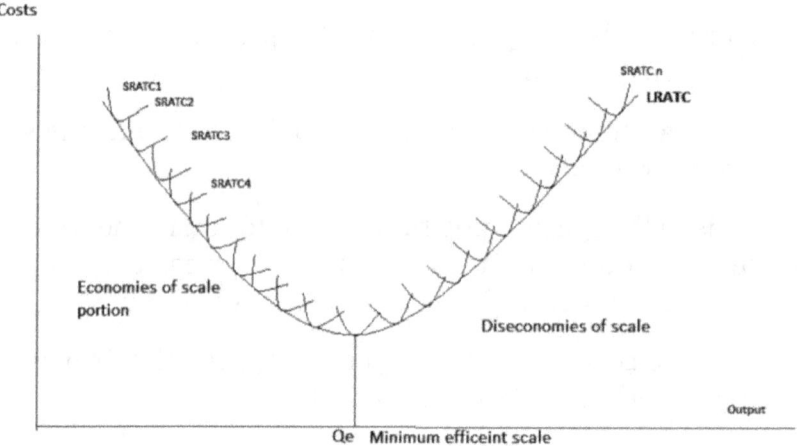

The area before the minimum efficient scale is economies of scale. The area after the minimum efficient scale is diseconomies of scale. At diseconomies of scale marginal cost are increasing while marginal revenues are decreasing. The diseconomies of scale may prevail due to managerial issues (managing larger scale of production may cause inefficiencies), politics involved in big firms, motivation problems with larger workforce.

A firm producing at level above than minimum efficient scale, need to reduce production to achieve Qe.

Points very near to Qe there may be constant return to scale. It means we may have flat LRATC curve there. Constant return to scale means constant costs and constant marginal return in that range.

## 2. Describe characteristics of perfect competition, monopolistic competition, oligopoly, and pure monopoly

We have four major types of market structures. These market structures can be differentiated with respect to following factors.

- Number of firms in the market
- Size of the firm
- Type of elasticity of demand
- Ways and degree of competition
- Ease of entrance into the market

**Perfect competition:** In this type of market structure large numbers of small firms are producing identical products. New firms are free to enter into the market. There are no barriers for entrance into business. Because of very small size of a firm they have no control over prices. They can sell their entire product at prevailing market prices. So the firms are price taker. And they have perfectly elastic horizontal demand curve. As the products are identical, firms only compete on the basis of prices. Market of agricultural products like wheat, rice can be a good example of perfect competition. The market forces of demand and supply determines the price.

**Monopolistic competition:** This is the market structure in which many sellers are selling differentiated products. These products are differentiated on the basis of quality, brand name, features or marketing strategies etc. As products are differentiated they are not perfect substitutes. Each firm has elastic (not perfectly elastic) downward demand curve. Also due to differentiated Products a small increase in prices would not make all customers to move away because people are brand conscious. As a result firm has some control over prices of their own product. Firms in this market structure make huge advertisement expenditure for their products to be more attractive. There are some barriers for new firm to enter into the market because the existing firms have occupied their customers who would not move to new products easily.

**Oligopoly:** This is the market structure where few but large producers are competing with each other. These firms may produce identical or differentiated products. As there are only a few number of firms in the market each firm considers the strategies and responses of other firms in setting their prices, quality and other features of the product. Each firm faces a downward sloping demand curve. Barriers to enter in the market are high. Operating system providers for smart phones, oil and gas Development Industry, auto industry are a good example of oligopoly. Google Android management must consider the Strategies and response of Apple iOS while making their own decisions. The competition in oligopoly market is based on prices brand name or product features.

*Monopoly:* This is a market structure where only one seller provides the whole supply of a product in the market and there is no close substitute of that product. The firm has full control over price or quantity. If a monopolist wants to sell more he can reduce prices and vice versa. So the firm faces download sloped demand curve. The demand curve of a firm is the demand curve of whole market. The monopolist can threat new firms to enter into the market so the barriers to entrance in the market are very high.

*A monopolist exists in the market due to any of the following reasons.*

- A monopolist can be protected by copyright or patents.
- Full control over critical resources can also create monopoly.
- Govt. policy can also be a cause of monopoly. In greater

public interest govt. creates monopolist. This happens in a situation where average cost of production is lower in some range of production. This is known as *natural monopoly*. Public utilities are typical example of natural monopoly.

- Some firms are so deeply penetrated in the markets it becomes almost impossible for other firms to complete with them. This is also a cause of monopoly. Changes in technology and consumer taste can reduce monopoly power.

Following table shows the main characteristics of each market structure.

| | Perfect Competition | Monopolistic competition | Oligopoly | Monopoly |
|---|---|---|---|---|
| Number of sellers | Large | Many | Few | Single |
| Pricing power | No | Some | Some to significant | Significant |
| Nature of competition | Price only | Price, huge marketing, Advertisement | Price, huge marketing, Advertisement | Not huge advertisement |
| Substitutes | Very close substitutes | Good substitute but differentiated products | Good substitute Or Differen-tiated products | No substitutes |
| Barriers to entrance | No | Low | High | Very high |

3: Explain supply and demand relationships under monopolistic competition, including the optimal price and output for firms as well as pricing strategy

4: Explain supply and demand relationships under oligopoly, including the optimal price and output for firms as well as pricing strategy

## Monopolistic Competition

If the following characteristics exist in the market the market is called monopolistic competition.

1. Large number of independent sellers.
2. Differentiated products are being sold in the market by sellers.
3. The competition is based on price quality and marketing.
3. Barriers to entry of new firms are low.
4. Sellers has some control over the prices of their own product

In monopolistic competition each firm faces downward sloping demand curve. This is mainly because when a firm increases its price the customers have options to move towards other products. That's why there pries elasticity is high.

As we have discussed in perfect competition, a firm in monopolistic competition is in equilibrium or can maximize its profits where marginal revenues are equal to marginal cost (MC=MR).

**Output decisions and equilibrium under monopolistic competition**

**Short run:**

In short run monopolistic competitive firm may earn economic profit, normal profit or normal loss.

When average total cost is less than average revenues (price) the firm earns economic profit as shown in the figure below.

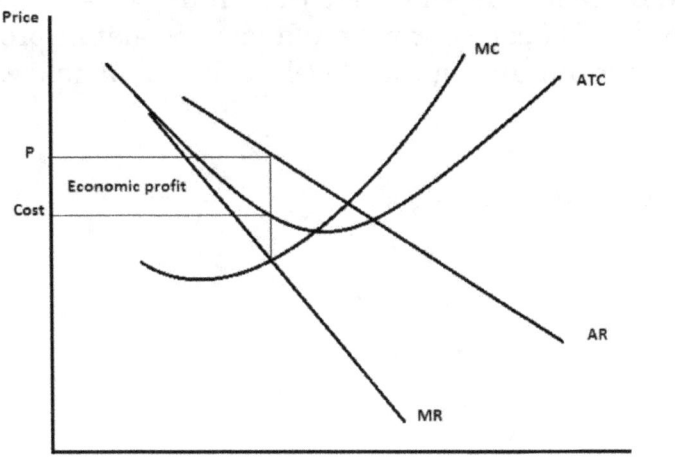

As we have discussed before when average total cost is just equal to price, firm earns normal profits. As shown in the figure below.

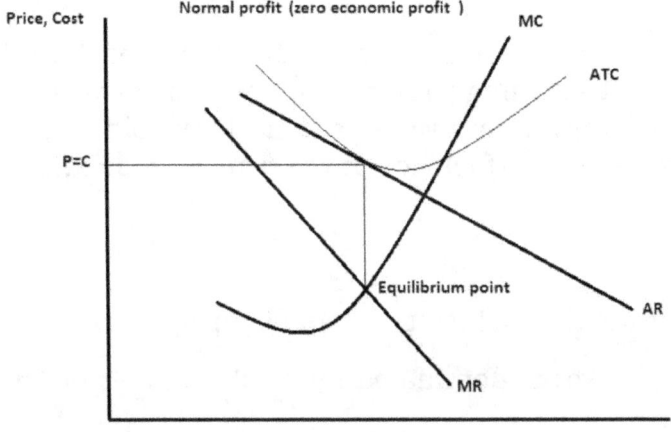

Same way if ATC is higher than price but AVC is below than price it is short run loss for the firm. Firm should continue its production in short run. Firm under monopolistic competition cannot earn abnormal loss because they have some control over price. Even short run normal loss is rare.

**Long run:** When in short run firm earns economic profit new firms enter into the market and share this profit. So in long run all firms in the market earn normal profit (zero economic profit). Long run equilibrium and output level is shown in following figure.

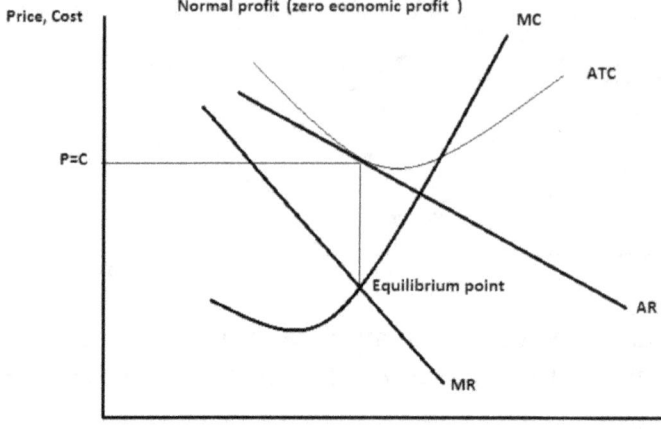

In monopolistic competition the price is always higher than the marginal cost. Another thing to remember here is average total cost is not at its minimum level at equilibrium point. Which means some productive inefficiency or the firm is producing less than its capacity.

## Oligopoly

Following are the characteristics of oligopoly market

1. The market is dominated by small number of large firms.
2. The firms either sell differentiated or identical products
3. Barriers to entry are high.

In this market structure all firms are interdependent. It means price changed by one firm will directly affect other firms. Due to complexity of oligopoly market, profit maximizing decisions, demand curve and pricing strategies can be described with the help of following models.

1. Kinked model demand curve model
2. Cournot duopoly model
3. Nash equilibrium (prisoner`s dilemma) model
4. Stackelberg dominant firm model

## Kinked model demand curve model

This model has following assumptions

1. The products are close substitutes.
2. The quality of products remains same throughout the analysis and firms do not spend on advertisement.
3. Each firm believes if it reduces the prices the competing firm will follow it but if it increases the prices the other firms will not follow it.

Every firm in the market faces more elastic demand curve (flatter) above a given price and less elastic (steeper) below that given price. (So there is a kink in the demand curve).

We can explain this with the help of following figure.

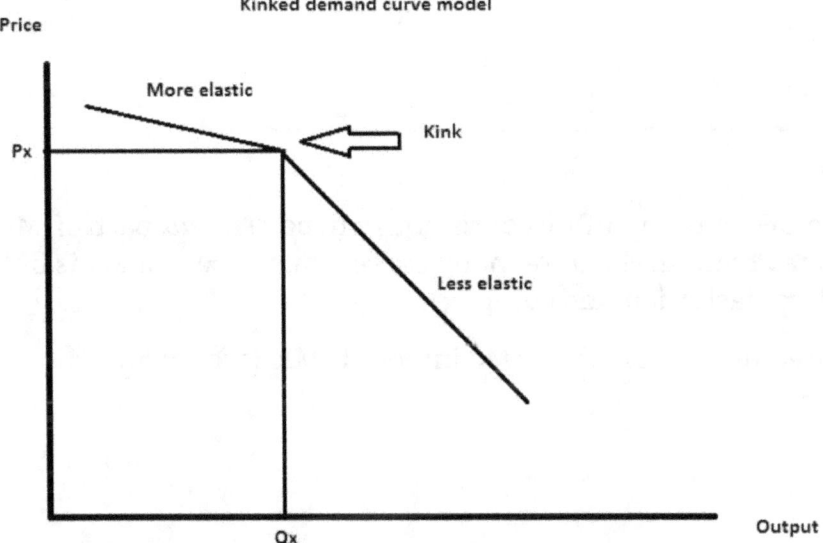

Kinked demand curve model

Px is kinked price and Qx is kinked quantity. Above that kinked price the firm faces more elastic demand curve. Therefore moving up from Px will cause the firm to lose the competition as the rival firm will not increase its price

On the other hand if the firm reduces its price from Px the rival firms will also reduce their price, and all the firms will face very little increase in their sales. So the Px is optimal price/ profit maximizing level and Qx is profit maximizing or optimal level of output.

**Marginal revenues under kinked demand model**

The MR curve is in discontinuous shape under this model.

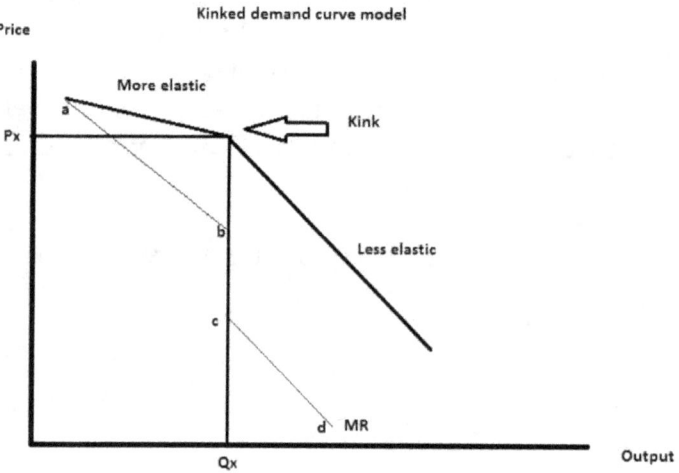

The MR curve is in discontinuous shape. The *ab* part of MR is related to more elastic demand curve while *cd* part of MR is linked to less elastic demand curve.

The equilibrium is where MC intersects MR as following

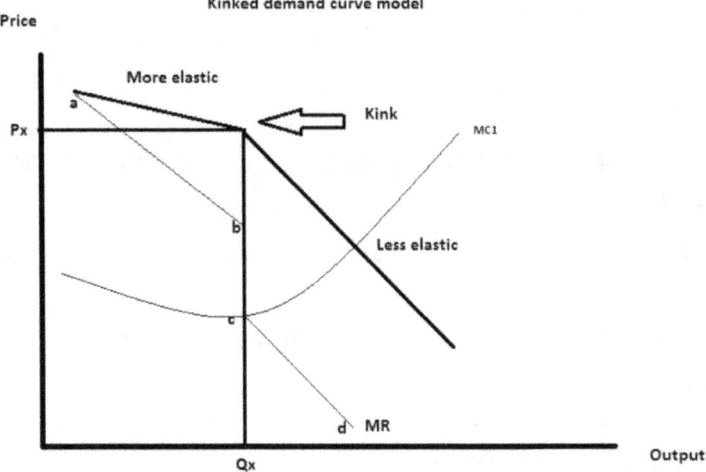

MC intersects the MR at point c. So the equilibrium point of output is Qx. Now if the cost increases marginal cost curve will move upward to MC 2. In this case the firm cannot increase its price because other firms will not increase their prices and our firm will lose its customers. Moreover the profits will remain same between the points *b* and *c*, so there is no motivation to increase the price. Therefore price and output will remain the same.

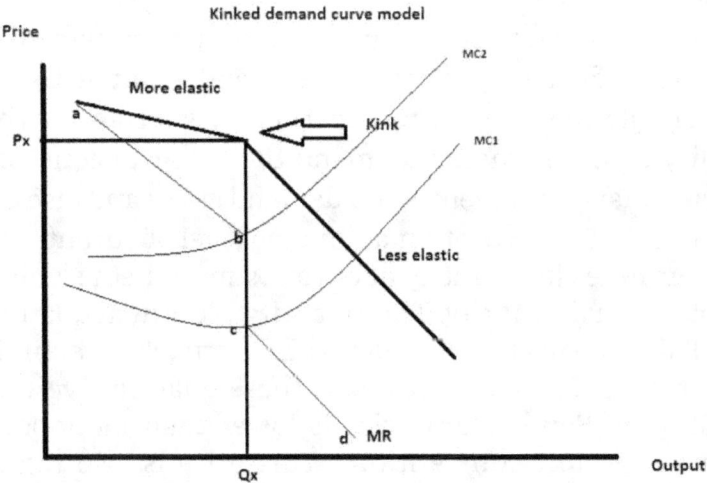

## Criticism on kinked model

This model is criticized by many economists on following grounds.

1. This model only emphasizes on price rigidity but does not explain determination of price.
2. The assumption of upward rigidity of prices is not true.
3. It ignores non price competitions like product differentiation, advertisement etc.
4. Model ignored price leadership and cartels effects.
5.

## Cournot duopoly model

It was developed by "A. Cournot" in 1838. Following are the assumptions of this model

1. There are two firms competing in the market (duopoly).
2. Both firms have identical and constant marginal cost curves.
3. Each firm knows the quantity of output provided by the other firm in previous period and assume that it will supply the same in next period. By subtracting that quality from the market demand the firm can construct its own marginal revenue and demand curve and also can determine its own profit maximizing level of output.

Each firm determines its quantity of output simultaneously until both firms have equal quantity. This quantity is optimal quantity of output. This means no one can gain from change in its quantity of output. This also means at these qualities we have stable equilibrium. Equilibrium price is lower than monopolist but higher than perfect competition. This price is also higher than marginal cost of the firms in duopoly. If more firms are added into this model the price gets lower and eventually becomes equal to marginal cost.

Cournot model is considered as the initial version of strategic game. Strategic game means the model in which best choices of one firm depends on the actions of other firms.

A better version of strategic game model is developed by john Nash, called Nash equilibrium.

## 5. Nash equilibrium (prisoner`s dilemma) model

John Nash developed this model. Nash equilibrium is obtained when no participant (firm) can gain (increase profit or decrease loss) by changing his own strategy when strategies of other participants (firms) are unchanged.

Prisoner`s dilemma is a standard example of Nash equilibrium in game theory. Two prisoners, prisoner 1 and prisoner 2, are believed to commit a serious crime. However it is very hard for prosecutor to prove the crime. So the prisoners are separated and offered following deal.

If Prisoner 1 confesses and Prisoner 2 remains quiet, Prisoner 1 goes free and
Prisoner 2 receives an 8 year sentence.
If Prisoner 2 confesses and Prisoner 1 remains quiet, Prisoner 2 goes free and
Prisoner 1 receives an 8 year sentence.
If both prisoners remain quiet, each will receive a 6-month sentence.
If both prisoners confess, each will receive a 2-year sentence.

Each prisoner can either betray other by confessing or coordinate by remaining silent. But no one knows what other is going to choose.

Following table shows the result of each outcome

|  | Prisoner 2 is quiet | Prisoner 2 confess |
|---|---|---|
| Prisoner1 is quiet | Prisoner 1 gets | Prisoner 1 gets 8 years |

| | | |
|---|---|---|
| | 6 months<br>Prisoner 2 gets<br>6 months | Prisoner 2 goes free |
| Prisoner 1 confess | Prisoner 1 goes free<br>Prisoner 2 gets 8 years<br>punishment | Prisoner 1 gets 2 years<br>Prisoner 2 gets 2 years<br>punishment |

It is clear from table that the best overall outcome for both prisoners is to remain quiet and get 6 month sentence. But this is not Nash equilibrium because each Prisoner can improve his situation from quiet/quiet by confessing. A quiet Prisoner can improve its situation by confessing and going free. Confess/confess is the **Nash equilibrium**, because in this situation no one can improve its position by changing the strategy.

Another and easy way to view this is that, no matter what other Prisoner is going to do the best strategy for each prisoner is to confess.

We can use this prisoner`s dilemma game for duopoly. As in prisoner`s dilemma Nash equilibrium is where both prisoners confess, in following example it's for both firms to cheat on each other. They agreed on a deal of collusive cooperation and charging high price. But each can earn extra profit by cheating.

| | Firm B cooperate | Firm B cheats |
|---|---|---|
| Firm A Cooperate | A earns economic profit<br>B earns economic profit | A earns loss<br>B earns extra economic profit |
| Firm B cheats | A earns extra economic profit<br>B earns loss | A earns normal (zero economic) profit<br>B earns normal (zero economic) profit |

Nash equilibrium is where both firms cheats and earn zero economic profit. Although the best strategy for each firm is to cooperate and honor the deal of charging high price. But each firm can improve its situation by cheating. If both cheat no firm can improve its situation by changing its own strategy.

LIBOR fixation, oil price fixations are some examples of collusive agreements but we saw that some firms occasionally cheated to obtain optimal profits. This cheating also comes from anti-trust laws by which govt. discourage cartels.

In collusive agreement to increase the prices and fewer tendencies to cheat happens when there are fewer firms in the market, producing similar products (more similar less cheating), and firms have similar cost structures, less competition from outside of cartel and severe retaliation from other firms if anyone cheats.

### 6. Stackelberg dominant firm model

In this model of oligopoly, there is a single dominant firm. The firm is dominant because of it lower cost structure and higher market share. This dominant firm set the price while other firms in the market follow this price. So the dominant firm is price setter and follower firms are price taker.

The dominant firm set the price according to its MC. Other firms have higher cost curves than dominant firms. They usually cannot charge lower price. If they do in short run the dominant firm can reduce its own price and other firms may be kicked out of the business because they will bear losses. In a result dominant firm believes the quantity supplied by other smaller firms will fall as price falls so the demand curve of dominant firm (DF) is related to the market demand as follows.

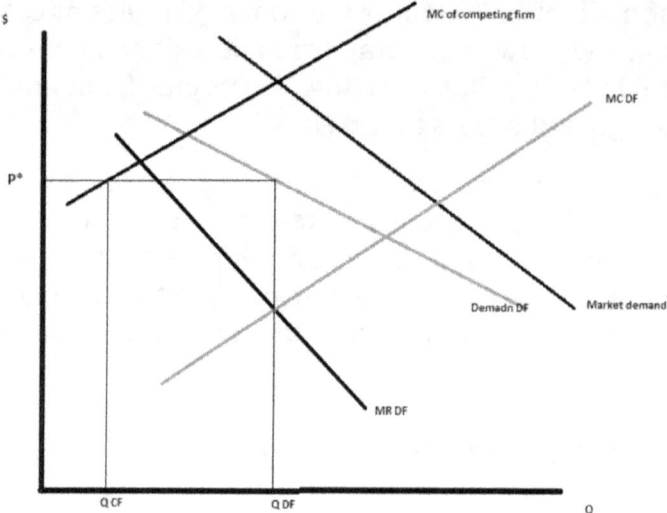

This is dominant firm (DF) oligopoly model. The DF will optimize its own profit at Q DF and P*. The competing firm will optimize its profit by producing quantity (QCF) equal to its MC.

## Pricing strategy under each market structure

**Monopolistic competition:** Under monopolistic competition profits are maximized by producing the quantity where marginal revenues are equal to marginal cost same as in another market structures. Firm operating under monopolistic competition faces downward sloping demand curve. Price would be higher than the marginal cost and marginal revenue.

**Oligopoly:** Under oligopoly the pricing and output decisions are interdependent on the decisions of other firms, the optimal pricing strategy will depend on what model we are considering.

1. *Kinked demand curve model: Under this model if a firm reduces its prices the competitive firm will also reduce its price but if a firm increase its price the competitive firm will not increase his price. Here the firm maximizes its profit by producing a quantity where its marginal cost is equal to marginal revenues. The marginal revenue*

*curve is discontinuous with kinked demand curve. In the discontinuous area the firm can produce its optimal level of output.*

2. **Cournot duopoly model:** *Each firm determinants its quantity of output in simultaneously until both firms have equal quantity. This quantity is optimal quality of output. This means no one can gain from change in its quantity of output. This also means at these qualities we have stable equilibrium. Equilibrium price is lower than monopolist but higher than perfect competition. This price is also higher than marginal cost of the firms in duopoly. If more firms are added into this model the price gets lower and eventually becomes equal to marginal cost.*

3. **Nash equilibrium (prisoner`s dilemma) model:** *Nash equilibrium is where both firms cheats and earn zero economic profit. Although the best strategy for each firm is to cooperate and honor the deal of charging high price. But each firm can improve its situation by cheating. If both cheat no firm can improve its situation by changing its own strategy.*

4. **Stackelberg dominant firm model:** *In this model of oligopoly, there is single dominant firm. This dominant firm set the price while other firms in the market follow this price. So the dominant firm is price setter and follower firms are price taker. The dominant firm set the price according to its MC. Other firms have higher cost curves than dominant firms. They usually cannot charge lower price. If they do in short run the dominant firm can reduce its own price and other firms may be kicked out of the business because they will bear losses. In a result dominant firm believes the quantity supplied by other smaller firms will fall as price falls so the demand curve of dominant firm (DF) is related to the market demand.*

**5: Identify the type of market structure within which a firm operates and describe the use and limitations of concentration measures**

We can identify the market structure within which a firm operates by using following characteristics

1. Number of firms in the industry
2. Nature of barriers to entry
3. Nature of substitutes available
4. Nature of competition
5. Pricing power of firm

We can understand this with the help of following table

|  | Perfect competition | Monopolistic competition | Oligopoly | Monopoly |
|---|---|---|---|---|
| Number of firms | Large number | Many firms | Few firms | Single firm |
| **Nature of barriers** | Free entry | Low barriers | High barriers | Very high barriers |
| Nature of substitutes available | Perfect or very good substitutes | Good substitutes but differentiated products | Close substitutes or differentiated products | No close substitute |
| **Nature of competition** | Only price | Price, marketing and features of products | Price, marketing and features of products | Low advertisement |
| **Pricing power of firm** | No power | Some power | Some to significant | Significant power |

Different measures are used to examine the pricing power of a firm in an industry.

These measures include elasticity of demand, percentage of market sales, and concentration measures. These measures are used to determine degree of monopoly/market power of a firm in the industry. Concentration measures are easier than elasticity measures. One most commonly used concentration measure is N-firm concentration ratio. Larger the concentration ratio less the competition is. This is calculated by summing percentage share of largest "n" firms in an industry. For example firm A has total sale to market sales (firm`s sales/market sales) of 20%. Firm B has 15%, firm C has 12%. N-firm concentration is calculated as 20+15 +12=37%.

This is very simple measure to calculate and understand but it also has drawbacks. It does not measure elasticity and market power directly. It also does not cover the mergers of different firms. This problem is eliminated by using alternative concentration ratio which is **Herfindahl-Hirschman Index** (HHI). This is calculated by sum of squares of market percentages of top n firms.

By using previous example we can calculate HHI as follows

$$20^2 + 15^2 + 12^2 = 769$$

The concentration measures also don't consider the barriers of entrance into the market. A firm might have huge market share but if market has lower barriers to enter into the market, the firm may not have the high pricing or market power.

# LEARNING MODULE 2

**UNDERSTANDING BUSINESS CYCLE**

### 1. Describe the business cycle and its phases

**Business cycle** is the ups and downs in economic activities or real GDP over the time around its growth Trend. A brief description of phases of business cycle is as follows;

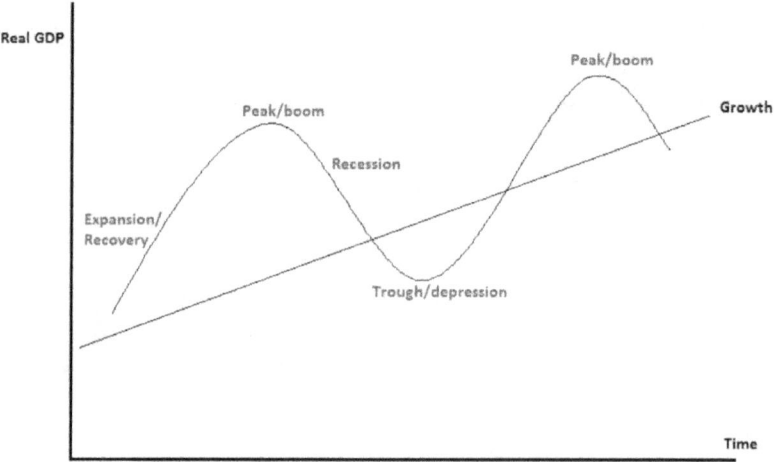

**Expansion/Recovery:** In this phase of business cycle the GDP is growing while unemployment is getting low and consumer`s spending are increasing.

**Peak/Boom:** At this stage the GDP is at its highest point. The employment is at its natural level.

**Recession:** During recession we see a reduction in economic activity like increase in unemployment while reduction in GDP.

**Depression:** Depression is the stage where economic activities are only nominal. Unemployment is at its highest level and GDP is at its lowest point.

The fluctuations in business cycle vary from some years to decades. The business cycles are most likely to occur in business dominant countries. The agricultural or highly state managed countries are less likely to face a business cycle.

## 2:Describe credit cycles.

The changing availability and cost of credit is referred to as a credit cycle. They depict the expansion of private sector credit, including loan availability and its consumption.

Lenders are more inclined to issue credit and on favorable conditions when the economy is improving. While, in a bad economic situation, lenders' willingness to extend credit will be limited, and the terms will be unfavorable, resulting in a drop in asset value and defaults and economic weakness. Credit cycle is a small part of financial or business cycle.

**Applications of credit cycle:**
Loose availability of credit to private sector can contribute towards financial crisis. This much availability of credit leads in making of real estate and asset pricing bubbles, which burst when the market realizes it weak fundamentals. Changes in access to external financing also lengthens the recession and other phases of business cycle i.e. expansion and contraction. Although credit cycle goes along with the business cycle, the credit cycle tends to be deeper, longer and sharper than business cycle.

Consequences for the policy: Investors must pay attention to credit cycle stage for the variety of reason such as;

- It help them to understand the changes in housing and construction sectors.

- It also help them to understand the magnitude of

business cycle expansion and contraction and what are the policy makers tend to do in each situation.

**3:** Describe how resource use, consumer and business activity, housing sector activity, and external trade sector activity vary over the business cycle and describe their measurement using economic indicators

### Resource Use

Inventories are considered very important indicator for business cycle. Businesses try to have adequate inventory in hand for smooth sales operations. When expansion phase of Business Cycle is near to its Boom the sales growth start getting slow. Means inventories are being accumulated. In this scenario inventory to sale ratio is above than its normal level. When businesses see they have more in their storage and sales are not increasing at very high speed they start decreasing their production. Reduction in production by most of the businesses is very important cause of contraction in later period. We know that in calculation of GDP we include inventories in GDP. By seeing only GDP we may expect Economic Strength in future while the economy is going to its contraction.

The aggregate demand decreases more when the firms start to reduce their cost by firing more employees and using less and less capital. With decrease in aggregate demand prices are getting lower and lower. And the economy reaches its trough. At trough the opposite happens. The prices are too low the people start buying more goods and services. As a result the aggregate demand starts to increase. The inventories are getting depleted more quickly and the inventory to sales ratio is lower than normal. To meet the market demand firms start to produce more. They need to hire more capital and labor. This is the economy entering into recovery or expansion again.

### Housing Sector

Housing sector follows the trends in business cycle and is

correlated with interest rate. Low interest rates encourage the consumers to buy mortgages.

If the future Expectations about the income and the consumer`s wealth is not very good people are not going to buy the mortgages and houses.

If a country has more people between 25 years to 40 years of age they tend to buy more houses and the construction activity increases.

**The External Trade Sector**

If demand for foreign goods increase the imports increase. Imports are highly dependent upon the domestic cyclical phase while exports depend on the external business cycle phase. If the domestic country is in expansion it demands more goods and services. The imports of that country increases. Near peak level the domestic currency is very much strengthened (with strengthened exchange rate) so the exports become very expensive for other countries. So in this phase imports increases but exports decreases. Due to decrease in the exports the domestic currencies start weakening which will subsequently make exports cheaper for other countries. And demand for domestic exports start to increase.

We have three types of economic indicators
1. Leading indicators   2.Coincident indicators    3. Lagging indicators

**1. Leading indicators:** Leading indicators are those indicators which may predict the business cycle. Average weekly work hours in manufacturing, new orders for consumer goods and non defense capital goods, housing permits, S&P 500 equity price index, Leading Credit Index, 10-year Treasury to Fed funds interest rate spread, average weekly claims for unemployment insurance and consumer expectations are some major leading indicators. These indicators should be paid special attention because they have the strong tendency to change ahead of Business Cycle.

**2. Coincident indicators:** These indicators changes during the business cycle progression. Real personal income, industrial production index are some coincident indicators.

**3. Lagging indicators:** Lagging indicators are changed after the economy has entered into a phase of Business Cycle. So these indicators confirm the prediction set by leading indicators. Average duration of unemployment, labor cost per unit, CPI, are some lagging indicators.

Organization for Economic Cooperation and Development (OECD) and Economic Cycle Research Institute (ECRI) publishes indexes for economic indicators for major economies. All these indicators should be analyzed together. If one or two leading indicators change their direction while other leading indicators are not, analyst should not predict a change in economic activities. Beware that these indicators have tendency but not exact relationship with business cycle.

# LEARNING MODULE 3

**FISCAL POLICY**

## Monetary policy

This is the policy used by the central bank to affect the quality of money supply and credit in the economy. Central Bank uses this policy to influence economic activities and price level in the economy. So the policy about money and credit supply is called monetary policy.

**Expansionary monetary policy:** It is also called accommodative or easy monetary policy. When central Bank uses different tools of monetary policy to increase the money and credit supply in the economy that is called expansionary monetary policy.

**Contractionary monetary**: It is also called tight or restrictive monetary policy. When Central Bank uses the monetary policy tools to decrease the amount of money or credit in the economy that is called contractionary monetary policy.

## Fiscal policy

This policy is in the hands of government. Government uses this policy to affect the economic activities and redistribution of wealth. This is the policy about government revenues and government spending (the government budget). The major portion of government revenues is Texas. When the revenues are more than spending the budget is called <u>surplus budget.</u> On the other hand when spending are more than revenues that budget is called <u>deficit budget</u>. When revenues and spending are same or equal that is called <u>balanced budget.</u>

**Expansionary fiscal policy:** When spending increases or taxes are lower it is called expansionary fiscal policy.

**Contractionary fiscal policy:** When taxes are more or spending or less that is called contractionary fiscal policy.

Both of these policies are used by their respective authorities to maintain economic stability, price level, economic growth and wealth distribution.

**2: Describe roles and objectives of fiscal policy as well as arguments as to whether the size of a national debt relative to GDP matters**

Fiscal policy means government's expenditures and revenues (mostly taxes) to influence economic activities. When the revenues are more than spending the budget is called <u>surplus budget.</u> On the other hand when spending are more than revenues that budget is called <u>deficit budget</u>. When revenues and spending are same or equal that is called <u>balanced budget.</u>

**Expansionary fiscal policy:** Expansionary fiscal policy means reduction in the taxes and or increase in the government spending.

**Contractionary fiscal policy:** Increase in taxes and or reduction in government spending is called contractionary fiscal policy.

## Role and objectives of fiscal policy

Expansionary fiscal policy is used to come out of a recessionary period. With this type of fiscal policy government spending is increased and taxes are reduces. Due to increase in government spending the aggregate demand increases. Reduction in taxes also increases the disposable income and the consumer demand increases. Both of these effects increases aggregate demand but budget deficit also increases.

On the same lines to slow the economic growth because the inflation rate is too high the government uses contractionary fiscal policy. This policy reduces the aggregate demand and also the budget deficit.

Fiscal policy can also be used for efficient resource utilization. A reduction in taxes encourages the investment. Moreover the higher taxes can be applied in sectors desired to be discouraged. In this way the resource mobilization and utilization can be optimized.

Fiscal policy also helps in removing income inequalities and disparities. In less developed areas a reduction in taxes helps improvement.

According to Keynesians the fiscal policy can affect the economy when it is operating at full employment level. Monetarists say monetary policy is more effective in inflation and the effects of fiscal policy in this regard are temporary.

When revenues of government are less than expenditures (budget deficit) the government borrows money. One popular way to calculate debt is total debt ratio which is total debt to GDP ratio because taxes (revenues) are linked to GDP. Total debt to GDP ratio must be within a certain limit. A higher of this ratio makes investors less confident about the country and the solvency of the country can be at stake. Public debt may not be always a bad sign depending on the nature of debt.

## Arguments in favor of fiscal debt relative to the GDP

1. If the debt is mostly consisted of the domestic borrowings it may not of serious concerns. Domestic borrowings are usually very cheap.
2. If the rate of real growth is greater than debt rate the debt will be depleted gradually. (Growth in taxes due to economic growth >Interest rate). It means the debt is being used for development purposes.
3. During recession if government wants to boost aggregate demand by borrowed spending, the borrowing of funds is

not bad. Deficit can take the country out of recessionary period.

## Arguments against of fiscal debt relative to the GDP

1. If the government has borrowed from international lenders it may of some serious concern if the debt to GDP ratio is higher.
2. If rate of real economic growth is less that the interest rate then the paying off back of debt would be a problem in future.
3. If the debt is not for development purposes but is used for current consumption and paying back of interest it is of serious concern.
4. If government has borrowed during recession but the country is stuck in recessionary period how the government will pay back the debt.
5. Crowding out effect: If government borrows that means the interest rate will go up. This will reduce the private borrowings and investment decreases.
6. Higher debt leads to higher future taxes so the economic activities can be reduced.
7. More indebted country losses the investor's confident.
8. At time of repayment of debt the government may print more money which can lead towards inflation (printing of new money is used to pay domestic debt).

3: Describe tools of fiscal policy, including their advantages and disadvantages.

Fiscal policy has two broad tools

1. Government revenues    2. Government spending

### Government revenues
Government collects its revenues in following forms
**Taxes:** Government collects taxes to manage state affairs and to influence the economic activities. Government collects taxes in

following forms

**Direct taxes:** These are the taxes deducted directly from the income or wealth. These are wealth tax, income tax, corporate tax, capital gain tax etc. These taxes help redistribution of income.

**Indirect tax:** These taxes are applied on goods/services. These taxes are levied to encourage/discourage consumption of certain goods/services. These taxes include sales tax, value added tax, excise tax etc.

Tax system is considered to be good if it efficient, simple, sufficient, and progressive.

## Government spending

Government spends on a number of goods/services as its fiscal policy tools. Following are major spending heads;

**Current expenditures/Non-development expenditures:** The routine (day to day) expenses of government are current expenditures. These expenditures are required for smooth and continuous working of the government at its current level. These expenditures are purchase of goods and services useable currently. These expenditures have no future impacts. Salaries of employees, stationary expenses and transfer payments are some examples.

## Capital Expenditures/ Development expenditures:

Expenditures to build an asset or to remove a liability are capital expenditures. When governments pay their loan, build dams, roads etc. These are called developmental or capital expenditures. These expenditures are made to increase the future efficiency of an economy.

## Advantages of fiscal policy

**Boost economic activities:** Fiscal policy can boost economic activities in a specific sector or region with reduction of taxes or increase in spending in that sector/region.

**Efficient use of scarce resources:** If some resources are very limited the government can tax on their uses so only efficient and most productive use of those resources can be increases.

**Quick results:** The fiscal policy creates more quick results than monetary policy.

## Disadvantages
**Political misuse:** Fiscal policy can be used by politicians and can be ineffective.
**Delayed implementation:** The application of direct taxes usually takes more time to implement so the results would be delayed.

Fiscal policy has two tools spending and revenues. These tools are used to attain economic objectives. For example in case of recession government decides to increase spending or lower the taxes to boost aggregate demand. With this people has more money and economy gets out of the lower demand and recessionary period. In case of boom period and high prices government increases the taxes or lower spending to decrease the aggregate demand. All these actions in fiscal policy are called discretionary fiscal policy.

**Fiscal policy does not necessarily give us the desired results due to following difficulties;**
1. *Wrong forecasts:* If the economic forecasts are not predicted correctly it means policy makers are going to make wrong decisions.
2. *Time lag:* It may take long time to government to understand the economic changes.

Fiscal policy is in government's hands. Sometimes it is politicized. Moreover the government has to vote for economic decisions. Meanwhile the economic conditions may have worsened.

Even after implementation it may takes sometimes to affect the economic indicators to change favorably.
3. *Crowding out:* The crowding out effect can make fiscal policy ineffective completely.
4. *Deficit financing:* If government is using expansionary

fiscal policy to boost aggregate demand it cannot increase the spending beyond a certain level. Eventually the government has to fill the deficit by foreign, local borrowing or by printing new money. Paying back the financed amount is also a problem and government has to implement higher taxes in near future or they will print new money. These two actions would worsen the situation ever more.

5. *Stagflation:* In case of stagflation (higher unemployment and inflation) the fiscal policy cannot address both problems simultaneously.

**Expansionary fiscal policy:** When spending increases or taxes are lower it is called expansionary fiscal policy. Budget deficit increases or surplus decreases with this type of policy.

**Contractionary fiscal policy:** When taxes are more or spending or less that is called contractionary fiscal policy. Budget deficit decreases or surplus increases with this type of policy.

# LEARNING MODULE 4:

**MONETARY POLICY**

**1: Describe roles and objectives of central banks.**

Following are some major roles of central bank

1. **Issuance of currency:** Central bank is the sole issuer of the currency of a country. No one else can do that. Traditionally the central bank backs some precious metal like gold to issue the currency. Later the banks used to back a reserve of the issued currency by gold, other metals or even foreign reserves to issue currency. Some central banks also issue currency without any back. That is called fiat money (the legal tender money).
2. **Bank of the government:** Central bank serves as government bank and provides consultation to the government.
3. **Banker of the banks:** The central bank also provides guidelines, regulate and supervise the other banks in the country.
4. **Monetary policy:** It is the central bank that issues and regulates the monetary policy in a country. Through monetary policy it can stabilize price level in country. It has many tools for monetary policy.
5. **Lender of last resort:** Whenever the other banks face shortage of funds due to any reason they can take loans from central bank. Central bank helps them to meet their short term requirement in case of emergencies.
6. **Holder of Gold and foreign exchange:** Central banks also

hold foreign reserves and gold for multipurpose.

7. **Payment system regularization:** Central bank makes rules and guidelines in the country for the safest and secured payment system in the country.

## Objectives of central bank

The main objective of central bank is to maintain price stability and target certain level of inflation. As zero inflation rate has never been a good idea for economic growth, maintaining some percentage of inflation has always been a target for the central bank. Inflation rate of 2 or 3 % is considered to be good for the health of an economy. Zero inflation can risk the economy for deflation.

The secondary objectives of Central Bank can be achieving full employment, maintain stability in exchange rate, sustainable economic growth and maintain a certain level of interest rate.

From secondary objectives maintaining a certain exchange rate is of most importance because a volatile exchange rate even when appreciated has certain problems for imports and exports of a country. One method is pegging the domestic currency with most traded foreign currency (like dollar). When dollar is getting higher value than their domestic currency they sell their foreign reserves of dollar to appreciate the domestic currency and vice versa (this act is called pegging). This act can risk increasing or decreasing of money supply.

2: Describe tools used to implement monetary policy tools and the monetary transmission mechanism, and explain the relationships between monetary policy and economic growth, inflation, interest, and exchange rates

## Tools used to implement monetary policy

Monetary policy is used by central bank with main objective to stabilize the price level. Following are some tools to implement this policy.

1. **Bank rate/Policy rate/Discount rate:** It is the rate

at which the central bank lends money to the other banks in its jurisdiction. If the rate is higher (lower) the borrowing banks` financing cost rises (falls) and the circulation money falls (rises). European central bank calls this refinancing rate.

Another way to apply this is central bank comes into agreement with other bank to buy their securities at lower price and will resell with higher price. The difference (percentage) is the interest rate (also called effective rate).

2. **Reserve requirement:** Banks are required to deposit certain percentage of their deposits into central bank. Increasing the reserve rate would reduce the funds available to lend and hence the money supply can be reduced.

3. **Open market operation:** This is another tool by which the central bank buys and sells the securities in open market. When the central bank wants to increase (decrease) money supply it buys (sells) the securities available in the market. This causes more (less) cash availability with investors and other economic agents and hence more (less) funds are available to lend.

**Monetary transmission mechanism:** This is a process by which changes in monetary policy especially the bank rate affects the price level and economy. Changes in policy rate can be transmitted to the price level and aggregate demand in following four ways

1. Short term interest rate      2. Asset's price
   3. Currency exchange rates               4. Expectations of economic agents

1. **Short term interest rate:** An increase or decrease in policy rate will increase or decrease the interest rates charged by other banks to its clients. Higher (lower) interest rate will

lead to less (more) demand for borrowed funds and reduce (increase) the aggregate demand.

2. **Asset's price:** Bonds, equity and other assets' value will decrease (increase) with increase (decrease) of interest rate as discount factor will increase (decrease). When prices of assets decreases people start saving more and consume less (wealth effect).

3. **Currency exchange rates:** Increase in interest rate will attract foreign investment in debt and interest bearing securities which will lead to appreciation of the domestic currency relative to the foreign currency and vice versa. We know that appreciation in domestic currency reduces the exports and it increases the imports.

4. **Expectations of economic agents:** With an increase (decrease) in interest rate households and businesses starts to consume less (more) because they have to adjust their decisions accordingly.

## Relationships between monetary policy and economic growth, inflation, interest, and exchange rates.

In short run monetary policy can affect the real economic growth, inflation, interest rate and exchange rate. The effects of monetary policy can be described as follows;

### Economic growth, Interest rate and aggregate demand

If central bank aims to increase real output it applies expansionary monetary policy. With expansionary monetary policy the interest rate is brought down. When interest rate is down borrowers are encourage to borrow more money while lenders (the banks) have more fund s to lend. Consequently the money supply increases and more businesses are developed/ expanded. Since consumers also avail the opportunity to borrow the overall aggregate demand increases.

The increase in aggregate demand also causes inflation and higher employment level.

Another way to see this is from wealth effect channel. Increase (decrease) in interest rate decrease (increases) the net wealth of the households and business. So they tend to decrease (increase) current consumptions.

**Effects on inflation**: In order to combat inflation the central bank uses contractionary monetary policy. With this policy interest rates are raised. Consequently the money supply decreases and so does the price level.

**Foreign exchange:** Domestic higher interest rate can attract foreign investment in interest bearing securities. With foreign investment domestic currency appreciates (other thing held constant) and vice versa.

On the other hand the inflation rate also affects the foreign exchange and we know that monetary policy directly hit the interest rate.

**3: Describe qualities of effective central banks; contrast their use of inflation, interest rate, and exchange rate targeting in expansionary or contractionary monetary policy; and describe the limitations of monetary policy**

### Qualities of effective central banks

The central bank of every country is responsible for price stability and inflation control. To perform these duties effectively it must has following qualities.

1. **Transparency:** Transparency means the central bank should publicize their views about economic environment and issue inflation reports. The central bank should also announce the policy rate and also why central Bank thinks this policy rate is required. The central bank should also be transparent in decision making process and other assessments. This quality of transparency leads towards credibility.

2. **Credibility:** The economic agents of a country must have confidence in the measures taken by Central Bank to

control inflation. To build this confidence central bank should have very high credibility. To create a sense of confidence central bank should follow their stated intentions.

3.          **Independence:** Central bank is independent if it is free from political influences. If central bank is under the pressure of political parties or government it cannot perform and target inflation effectively. Sometimes Central Bank has to take hard decisions which a government or political party cannot take. During that time if the central bank is influenced by politics it will not go well for the economy.

## Use of inflation, interest rate, and exchange rate targeting by central banks

**Interest rate targeting:** Central bank targets interest rate by increasing or decreasing money supply and monetary growth in the country.  Monetary authority increases the money supply when the interest rate is above than desired. On the other hand central bank reduces the money supply when the interest rate in below than required.

**Inflation targeting:** This is the most common practice and legal requirement in most of the countries. Instead of targeting interest rate the central bank targets the inflation rate usually from 1% to 3% by changing interest rate. We have seen the effects of changes in interest rate on the inflation in monetary policy.

**Foreign exchange rate targeting:** The exchange rate is also being targeted in most of the economies now-a- days for smooth exports and imports growth.  When domestic currency is depreciated in relative to foreign currency (usually dollars) the central bank sells its foreign reserves to appreciate domestic currency and vice versa. This is called pegging. This method also has limitations. For example if the foreign reserves are depleted but still required exchange rate are not achieved. Additionally the foreign reserves are also needed for the foreign payments.

## Limitations of monetary policy

Although the monetary policy is used for inflation and money supply control but sometimes it does not produce intended results.

**Deflation:** In case of lower demand monetary authorities try to boost aggregate demand by lowering the policy rate. But in case of deflation the central bank can lower the interest rate to zero even then the aggregate demand cannot be boosted. Now there is no other option remains with the central bank to increase aggregate demand.

**Underdeveloped countries with barter system:** In many underdeveloped countries there is large sector especially in rural areas where transactions are being held in barter system. What a central bank and its monetary policy can do where there is no money.

**Underdeveloped money market:** Monetary policy is ineffective or less effective in countries where money market is not much developed. For example if there is an economy where there are not stocks, bonds and bills monetary policy cannot play its role.

**Most liquid banks:** When commercial banks have more funds, it means they are not borrowing from the central bank and the policy rate cannot affect their lending to clients.
Foreign banks also make the monetary policy ineffective. In case of tight monetary policy they withdraw cash from their head offices making the policy rate ineffective.

**Money held as cash:** When people held more money as cash and less in banks they will less likely to borrow from banks and the policy rate cannot affect them. This practice is very common in underdeveloped and developing countries.

**Uncertainty:** When economic agents are not sure about the country`s future they prefer to hold more cash. Holding cash makes monetary policy ineffective.

**Liquidity trap:** Liquidity trap is a situation where interest rate is low and people save more and avoid purchasing bonds in a hope that in future the interest rate will rise. This act makes monetary policy ineffective.

## 4: Explain the interaction of monetary and fiscal policy.

Both monetary and fiscal policies can be expansionary and contractionay. With their interaction followings four outcomes are possible.

**Expansionary fiscal and monetary policies:** With both expansionary policies a great boost in the economy occurs. With lower taxes and higher government spending the businesses would produce more while with lower interest rate the borrowing cost falls and investment increases. Both policies will make higher consumption and use of consumer as well as capital goods. So the unemployment decreases and price level rises.

**Contractionary fiscal and monetary policies:** The aggregate demand and GDP level will be lower due to contractionary fiscal policy while interest rate rises. Hence the cost of borrowing increases. Consequently public and private sector contracts and the price level falls.

**Contractionary fiscal policy and expansionary monetary policy:** The interest rate will fall due to expansion in money supply while aggregate demand will partly decrease due to less government consumptions. But the private sector aggregate demand will rise (household and businesses) because cost of borrowing is low. So the net effect would be expansion of private sector. The net effect on GDP could be positive or negative depending on the portion of government and private sector in GDP. If G is more than C plus I the GDP will fall and vice versa.

**Expansionary fiscal policy and contractionary monetary policy:** This is exactly opposite of above case. The aggregate demand will rise due to higher government spending while the interest rate is high due to tight monetary policy. The private sector (household and businesses) would contract. The net effect on GDP could be positive or negative depending on the portion of government and private sector in GDP. If G is more than C + I the GDP will rise and vice versa.

The net effect also depends on the multiplier effect. Usually the fiscal multiplier is higher than monetary multiplier.

# LEARNING MODULE 5

**INTRODUCTION TO GEOPOLITICS**

1: Describe geopolitics from a cooperation vs competition perspective.

Geopolitics refers to the impact of geography and politics. It explores how geography influences relations between countries and regions. Geopolitics examines the connections between regional governments, groups, organizations, and financial institutions. It seeks to understand how these factors interact and shape national and international relations.

Geopolitical risks refer to the dangers that arise from tensions and actions taken by any of the parties mentioned above, which can directly or indirectly disrupt or hinder the normal and peaceful development of international relations. These risks can include terrorist attacks, robberies, natural disasters, legislative changes, or conflicts of interest between parties.

Geopolitics also impacts interest rates, market stability, and economic growth. Since geopolitical factors can alter key economic indicators, their influence on investments is inevitable. They can affect the expected return and risk associated with an asset. Therefore, when developing an investment strategy for a client, an analyst should consider the implications of geopolitics.

These individuals and groups can either work together or act independently, depending on their own interests or the interests of their country.

Types of actors:

State actors: State actors act on a government's behalf. This includes all government bodies and individuals associated with the government.

Non-state actors: These are influential individuals or groups that have a significant impact on political, economic, international relations, or financial activities but are not aligned with any government authority. Examples of non-state actors include NGOs, multinational corporations, and charitable groups.

**Cooperative and Non-Cooperative Relations**

When actors come together for a shared purpose, it is known as cooperative relations.

Common reasons for cooperation include:

**National security**: State actors join forces for the sake of the protection of their people and country from external threats. Cooperative geopolitics helps in enhancing national security.

**Economic reasons:** Countries collaborate to promote international trade of goods and services, aiming to benefit their respective economies.

**Resource acquisition:** Cooperation among actors allows them to work together in obtaining and utilizing valuable resources.

**Soft power projection:** States use geopolitics to display a positive and favorable image to the world.

On the other hand, non-cooperation occurs when states and other actors choose not to collaborate due to conflicting national interests. In such cases, non-cooperation is considered more advantageous than cooperation.

2: Describe geopolitics and its relationship with globalization.

Globalization is the process of connection and integration between people, organizations, and governments worldwide. On the other hand, anti-globalization or nationalism refers to a country prioritizing its own economic interests, even if it means disregarding or conflicting with other countries. Additionally, there is a form of globalization that occurs on a smaller scale, known as microeconomic globalization. This involves producing goods in one country using materials from another and then selling those goods in different countries under various brand names and qualities. It is a frequent occurrence for products to be produced in one country by utilizing parts from various countries, assembled in a different country, and ultimately marketed and sold in a third country.

Globalization often stems from economic collaborations. Individuals and companies seeking profit explore opportunities outside their home country to produce, manufacture, and sell products in different regions. The main motivations behind globalization are increasing profits, reducing costs, accessing resources, and entering foreign markets.

However, globalization also comes with certain costs, including:

- Interference in other countries affairs
- Brain drain, which refers to the migration of skilled individuals from developing countries to wealthier nations
- Income inequality
- Challenges in governance due to the involvement of multiple states.

Different countries have varied responses to globalization. Here is a general overview of how states have reacted to globalization and its impact on international relations and geopolitics.

**Autarky:** Some countries opt for autarky, which means they have limited foreign trade and minimal external debts. These countries strive to be self-sufficient and have complete control over their own products, services, and technology. They are often referred to as closed economies. While these countries may experience steady growth initially, over time, the rate of progress tends to diminish.

**Hegemony:** Hegemonic states assert their control over resources and act as regional or global leaders. They demonstrate political and economic dominance over other countries. Countries that have cooperative agreements with these leading powers can benefit from the advantages of hegemony. However, when the hegemonic influence declines, geopolitical risks start to emerge.

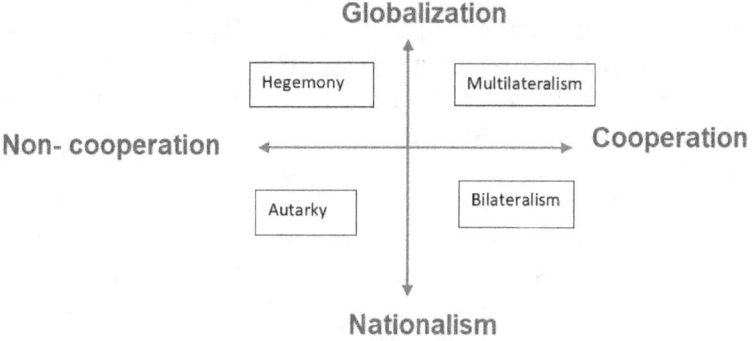

**Globalization, actrs and associated risks**

## Multilateralism

Certain countries engage in mutually beneficial trade agreements, allowing their corporations to participate in global networking and trade. This involvement in multilateralism grants these countries access to international resources and enables them to optimize their utilization. However, it also leads to interdependency among nations, exposing them to geopolitical risks.

**Bilateralism** refers to the collaboration between two countries in areas such as politics, economics, finance, or culture.

3: Describe functions and objectives of the international organizations that facilitate trade, including the World Bank, the International Monetary Fund, and the World Trade Organization

The world economy is complex and getting even more complex. To work in coherently, cooperation between the countries is essential. For that purpose, different organizations come into the picture. The world trade organization, IMF and World Bank.

## Word Bank:

Countries collaborate with the World Bank to achieve global economic equilibrium. The World Bank is a global lender and development partner that provides loans, funds, and technical assistance to low-income nations to overcome poverty and achieve sustainable development. Its primary goal is to facilitate the expansion and prosperity of national economies. Professionally sponsored and supervised initiatives in infrastructure, education, healthcare, and agriculture assist us in accomplishing this objective. This contributes to poverty reduction by providing developing countries with the resources necessary to establish a more promising future.  It supports projects in agriculture, education, healthcare, and infrastructure, and assists in enhancing economic policies and processes. The bank also supports initiatives aimed at preserving the environment and making people more resilient to climate change. It collaborates with governments, civil society organizations, and the private sector to contribute significantly to many nations' economic development.

World Bank was established in December 1945 to help the devastated countries from World War II to reconstruct.

World Bank assists its member countries to promote foreign investment, helps in their balance of payment issues, provides low interest loan for short and long run growth and development projects. They also help the middle income nations to get out of the extreme poverty. World Bank also provides guarantees for the member countries for loan and foreign investments.

## International monetary fund (IMF)

IMF does following for its member countries

- It promotes international monetary cooperation.
- It facilitates the international trade
- It helps to maintain stable exchange rate.
- It helps the international payments and tries to eliminate payment restrictions.
- Provides short term funds for adjustments in balance of

payment.

- It also provides consultation for its member countries.

**World Trade Organization (WTO)**

According to WTO they do following (more at WWW.WTO.ORG)

The World Trade Organization (WTO) is the only global international organization dealing with the rules of trade between nations. At its heart are the WTO agreements, negotiated and signed by the bulk of the world's trading nations and ratified in their parliaments. The goal is to ensure that trade flows as smoothly, predictably and freely as possible.

## 4: Describe geopolitical risk

Geopolitical risk refers to the possible negative impacts on economic and business activities, such as disruptions in international trade, investments, and supply chains. Geopolitical risk encompasses several factors such as political instability, interstate conflicts, trade disputes, cyber warfare, and the consequences of climate change. Possible consequences of these risks include supply chain disruptions, increased expenditures, and damage to the brand's image.

Trade disputes and protectionism may result in increased expenses and greater obstacles for businesses attempting to enter certain markets. The increasing reliance on technology has resulted in an escalation of cybersecurity issues, such as data breaches and theft of intellectual property. Supply chains and corporate operations may be affected by climate change and natural catastrophes.

Geopolitical risks have several consequences, such as interruptions in supply chains, higher expenses resulting from tariffs, insurance premiums, and security measures, harm to reputation owing to engagement in contentious geopolitical events, and operational challenges caused by trade restrictions and regulatory changes.

Companies may mitigate their vulnerability to geopolitical risk via several measures such as insurance, crisis management, diversification, risk monitoring, and political risk analysis. Organisations may enhance their financial gains and bolster their ability to withstand geopolitical risk by acquiring knowledge about it and then implementing appropriate risk management strategies.

## 5: Describe tools of geopolitics and their impact on regions and economies

Geopolitical tools are the means used by geopolitical actors to advance their interests in relation to others.

i. Tools for national security

State actors exert direct or indirect control to gain access to resources, people, and/or boundaries. National security instruments might either be operational or only potential hazards.

These tools can be used to destruct the physical infrastructure or to restrict the migration from armed.

ii. Financial tools

Financial tools can also be cooperative or non-cooperative. Cooperative might include free cross border currency movements, exchange rates and investments. Non-cooperative is opposite and may include of restriction in currency movements and investments. Collaborations in these tools can reduce geopolitical risk while non-cooperative can cause this risk. These measures can play their role in other country`s system. As most of the countries trade in USD, a change in USD interest rates and policy rates can affect other countries.

These tools are usually used as multi-tools approach.

## 6: Describe impact of Geopolitical risk on investments

Geopolitical Risk: A Danger to Investments
Geopolitical risk creates uncertainty and can affect investments. It stems from political choices, happenings, or shifts that sway investment decisions. Picture driving on a misty road with poor visibility where sudden bends might cause crashes.
How Geopolitical Risk Has an Impact on Investments
Market Volatility: Geopolitical tensions and conflicts often cause stock prices, exchange rates, and commodity prices to fluctuate more. This creates a tough environment for investors.

Investment Deterrence: Political instability, trade disputes, and policy shifts can stop investors from putting money into certain regions or industries. This has an impact on money flowing out of the country and slowing down the economy.

Higher Expenses: Companies often deal with increased costs due to geopolitical dangers like pricier insurance, supply chain troubles, and safety precautions. These expenses can reduce profit margins.

Business Hurdles: Geopolitical happenings can upset how companies operate causing production holdups, supply chain issues, and harm to their image.

Unclear Rules: Shifts in government policies, trade regulations, and tax laws can create confusion for investors and influence their choices to invest.

Examples of Geopolitical Danger

Trade fights: Taxes and trade restrictions can disrupt global supply chains and raise costs for businesses.

# LEARNING MODULE 6

**INTERNATIONAL TRADE**

1: Describe benefits and costs of international trade.

## The benefits

1. **Availability of goods:** With the help of international trade more variety of a specific good is available. Those goods which are not being produced are available to the consumers. So the living standard increases.
2. **Efficient resource allocation:** According to the theory of comparative advantage the countries can allocate their resources for production of those goods/services in which they are most efficient and can import other products. This enables them to allocate their resources more efficiently.
3. **Cost reduction and efficient production:** In order to remain competitive in international market, countries tries to adopt more efficient way of production and reduce their costs. Otherwise they would be out of the market.
4. **Apprehension of shortage can be eliminated:** With more availability of goods the fear of shortage is eliminated.
5. **New markets and international growth:** When goods can be exported internationally the new markets are available for domestically produced goods. Take an example of china. They have been growing due to their huge share in exports. Also the surplus production can be exported and get revenues. So the fear of overproduction is also

eliminated.

## Cost or disadvantages of international trade

1. **Political risk:** When a company is mainly exporting to a specific country any changes in politics of that country can harm the exports.

2. **Exchange rate risk:** In imports and exports we are dealing with foreign currencies relative to domestic country. Any change in exchange rate will affect the revenues and trade. For example if domestic currency is appreciated the exports becomes dearer for other countries. And if domestic currency is depreciated the imports become dearer. Also the revenue increases/decreases with changes in exchange rate.

3. **Dependency:** If a country is importing a very sensitive good, crucial for the survival or growth of that county, and the exporting country stops the supply the importer country can be at great risk. For example imports of oil and Weapons.

4. **Domestic industry can be discouraged:** If a country starts importing a good and its domestic industry is not competitive enough to face foreign competition then the firms will be closed and the people will be unemployed working in that industry.

Even if local firms try to compete they need to use capital intensive production methods. This also makes people to lose their job.

Depending on the nature of the country and other policies the international trade can be of greater benefits than being without international trade.

2: Compare types of trade restrictions, such as tariffs, quotas, and export subsidies, and their economic implications.

Some countries impose trade restrictions. These restrictions are supported by some economists while other economists oppose them. The main reasons to impose restriction are to support infant domestic industries, for national security, and employees' job protection.

## Types of trade restrictions

**Tariffs:** These are the taxes imposed on imports.

**Licensing:** Licenses are granted to a specific business to import a specific product. Licensing increase the prices of products.

**Quotas:** These are imposed to limit the amount of imports.

**Export subsidies:** Subsidies are given to the exporters to encourage exports and make them competitive in international markets.

**Content requirement:** A restriction imposed by the government that minimum domestic contents must be included in production of a certain product or even a service.

**Voluntarily export restraints (VERs):** These are the restrictions imposed by exporting country to limit its exports to avoid the import restriction that may be imposed by its importing country. Usually these restrictions are imposed on request of importing partner country.

## Economic implications of trade restrictions

We are to examine the effect of each restriction.

**Tariff:** When tariff is imposed on imports the prices of imported goods rises domestically. Consumption of locally goods increases. So the domestic producer gains while the international producer loses. Government gains from the tariff.

**Licensing:** Licensing increases the prices while government gains. If licensing is imposed on a product which can be used negatively government can save the society. Again the govt. gains from the licensing fee.

**Quotas:** Quotas restrict the amount of imports. The domestic consumer lose, international producer lose while the domestic producer gain from it.

**Export subsidies:** Government provides some subsidies to exporters. The local producers gain as their products are going abroad but local consumers lose as the prices go up. Foreign consumer gains as they have more variety of goods while the foreign producer loses due to competition.

**Content requirement:** Local producer of those contents gains while the producer of goods is somewhat negatively affected. Foreign and local consumers may be affected by getting somewhat lower quality of goods (if the contents are of high quality they would have been used without any restriction).

**Voluntarily export restraints (VERs):** The exporter loses while the consumers of foreigner country also lose.

The overall effects of trade restrictions are decrease in consumer surplus, increase local producer's surplus, increase price and decrease quantity of supply.

## Capital restrictions

These are the measures taken by the governments to control or restrict the capital outflow. These measures can include the taxes on the income earned by foreign investors, restrictions on excess inflow and outflow of foreign investment, tariffs, volume restrictions etc. These restrictions helps the governments in short run to avoid excessive outflows of capital in recessionary or correction period of domestic country and also to protect domestic newborn uncompetitive industries from foreign competition (foreign more efficient companies are restricted to enter into 1omesticc market by restricting the foreign investment). The consumers lose as the prices goes up while government gains from tariffs. So in long run the costs are more than benefits. But these restrictions are helpful mostly for underdeveloped and developing countries.

**3: Explain motivations for and advantages of trading blocs, common markets, and economic unions.**

There are many trade agreements between countries to reduce trade barriers. These agreements increase the trade among member countries so the overall welfare increases. However trade agreements reduce the trade between non member countries and if member countries are selling dearer goods (than non member countries) the welfare can decrease.

## Trading blocs
A trading bloc means some geographically connected nations come together to increase trade and to restrict trade with non member countries.

If they made a free trade agreement it means all restrictions on imports and exports among member countries are removed. Some agreements also include common type of restriction with non member countries.

Asia-Pacific Economic Cooperation (APEC) and the Association of Southeast Asian Nations (ASEAN) are some examples. These agreements enable the member countries to increase their welfare.

## Common markets
All restrictions on imports and exports among member countries are removed.

Member countries adopt a common type of restriction with non member countries.

All barriers to movement of labor and capital among member countries are removed. For example East African Common Market.

## Economic Unions
All restrictions on imports and exports among member countries are removed.

Adopt a common type of restriction with non member countries.

All barriers to movement of labor and capital among member countries are removed.

Common institutions and common economic policies are established among member countries.

For example European Union.

## Motivations and Advantages

Following can be some motivation and advantages for trading blocs, common markets, and economic unions.

1. Entry into new markets.
2. Increase in the resource availability
3. Future competition can be reduced by gaining competiveness
4. Reduction of trade barriers.
5. Gain economies of scale.

# LEARNING MODULE 7

**CAPITAL FLOWS AND FX MARKET**

1: Describe the foreign exchange market, including its functions and participants, distinguish between nominal and real exchange rates, and calculate and interpret the percentage change in a currency relative to another currency

## Foreign exchange market

The market in which the currencies of different countries are exchanged and the exchange rates are determined is called the foreign exchange market.

## Functions of foreign exchange market

In absence of foreign exchange market the international trade is almost impossible. Residents of different countries trade goods and services in different countries. For this they need foreign currency which is available in foreign exchange market.

Larger portion of transactions in foreign exchange market is financial market transactions (flow of capital). Investors use foreign exchange market to convert currencies to invest in other countries.

When the parties involved in foreign market feels risk (of movement of exchange rate unfavorably) they enter into forward currency exchange contract (as we have discussed in previously). Other contracts of foreign exchange market to hedge risk include foreign exchange swaps (FX swaps), FX options, and outright forward contracts (we will discuss them later in other volume).

Some participants try to speculate the exchange rate and purchase some currency (they think is undervalued) and sell it when it appreciates and get benefits.

**Participants in the Foreign Exchange Market**
The foreign exchange market participants are of two types the buy side and sell side. The sell side is consisted with large multinational banks. On the buy side there are clients of these banks who use these banks to undertake transactions. The buy side participants include following;

**Corporations/corporate account:** Multinational corporations do business in different countries through FX market. They hedge exchange rate risk by hedging.

**Investment account:** Parties involve in investment in securities of other countries. They hedge or speculate using currency derivatives. Two broad types of investment account are real money accounts and Leveraged accounts. **Real money accounts:** These are the cross-border investments in mutual funds, pension funds etc. These accounts do not use derivatives. **Leveraged accounts** investment accounts with use of derivatives.

**Government:** Government also uses FX market for foreign transactions like buying/selling military equipments.

**Central banks:** Central banks use FX market to maintain a certain level of exchange rate. They also use foreign currencies to pay the imports bills.

**Individuals and small entities:** Households also do FX transactions to convert currencies in order to go to a foreign country they need foreign currency etc. Small entities like tourism firm also need FX market.

**Distinguish between nominal and real exchange rates**

**Exchange rate:** The value of one currency in terms of another country is called exchange rate. For example 1.15 Dollars for 1 euro. We will write 1.15Dollar per one euro or $1.15/1 € or 1.15 USD/EUR.

In this example the dollars is price currency while euro is base currency. 1.15 dollars is the price of base currency in terms of price currency. The price / base currency is quotation is direct quote for the residents of price currency while this is indirect quote for the residents of base currency.

**Nominal exchange rate:**  Number of units of the domestic currency that can purchase a unit of a foreign currency is called nominal exchange rate. For instance 1.15USD/euro is nominal exchange rate as it tells residents of USA they need 1.15 dollars to buy one unit of euro.

**Real Exchange rate:** Real exchange rate tells us how many goods/services of domestic country can be exchanged with goods/services of foreign country (while the nominal exchange rate tells us how much domestic currency units can be exchanged with the one unit of foreign currency).

Real Exchange rate = Nominal exchange rate x $\frac{price\ level\ in\ base\ currency}{Price\ level\ in\ foreign\ country}$

For price level we normally use CPI.

Real exchange rate is of more concern with imports and exports than nominal exchange rate. When real exchange rate is high the relative prices of home country are higher than foreign price level. So exports are dearer for other countries while imports are cheaper for the domestic residents. As a result net imports increases. In contrast when real exchange rate falls, net exports increases.

**Spot exchange rate:** An exchange rate applicable in case of immediate delivery. By immediate delivery mostly means delivery after two days of transaction.

**Forward exchange rate:** An agreed exchange rate between parties to exchange specific amount of currencies in future date.  These forward contracts are of mostly 30 days, 60 days, 90 days, or one year. These contracts are made when a party (or a firm) need a currency in future but fears that the exchange rate will move unfavorably. By getting into forward contract the firm is saving its position against exchange rate risk (also called hedging of risk).

For example a USA firm is entering into contract with a British firm to exchange USD with British pound at a rate of 1.28USD/£.

## Calculation and interpretation of the percentage change in a currency relative to another currency

Let`s say the exchange rate between USD and Euro changed from was 1.15USD/Euro to 1.45 USD/Euro. The percentage change in USD for Euro is calculated as

$\frac{1.45}{1.15} - 1 = 26.08\%$.

It means the Euro is appreciated by 26.08 % relative to USD as it can buy 26.08% more dollars.

It also means that the USD is depreciated relative to Euro but we cannot say the depreciation in USD is 26.08%. To calculate depreciation in USD we need to convert the quote USD/Euro to Euro/USD. So the initial exchange rate now is 1/1.15 = 0.869 and second quote is 1/1.45 =0.689. Now calculate percentage change as

$\frac{0.869}{0.689} - 1 = 26.12\%$

In our example the difference is slight but it can be much more so always calculate the appreciation/depreciation carefully. <u>Always remember we can calculate the percentage change (appreciation/ depreciation) of base currency in a quotation.</u>

2: Describe exchange rate regimes and explain the effects of exchange rates on countries' international trade and capital flows

## Exchange rate regimes

There are two broad categories of exchange rate regimes. 1. Countries who do have or do not use their own currency       2. Countries with their own currency.

### 1. Countries who do have or do not use their own currency

These countries use either dollarization or are in a monetary union where most of the transactions are done in a common currency.

*Dollarization:* When a country does not issue its own currency they use the currency of another country. That country cannot own a monetary policy. Ecuador, East Timor, El Salvador are some countries who use dollar and do not have their own currency.

*Monetary union:* This is a union in which member countries use common currency over their domestic currencies. European Union is the example of monetary union. Each member country cannot issue the monetary policy but participates to determine common monetary policy with European Central bank.

### 2. Countries with their own currency

Following are some practices done by the countries with their own currency.

*Currency board arrangement:* A board is established which ensures fixed exchange rate. In this arrangement a specific amount of domestic currency is being exchanged with a specific amount of foreign currency. For example Bulgaria and Hong Kong use this arrangement. Through this arrangement the domestic currency is only issued if it is fully backed by foreign currency like US dollars. These countries cannot manipulate the interest rate and money supply. They usually import interest rate and inflation from foreign currency (backed currency). These countries use their foreign currency to purchase interest bearing securities of foreign currency and earn interest.

*Conventional fixed peg arrangement:* In this arrangement countries maintain a certain exchange rate (called pegging) with a margin of +-1% with another currency (or basket of major trading currencies like dollar, Euro, Yen etc). These countries issue their own currency, have their own monetary policy so they can manipulate interest rate and inflation. Qatar, Oman, Bahrain use USD to peg the exchange rate.

*Target zone:* Just like conventional peg but with higher margin of +-2. It gives the countries more flexibility for monetary policy.

*Crawling peg:* The exchange rate is adjusted periodically usually to adjust for inflation. It can be active crawling or passive crawling peg. Nicaragua uses crawling peg.

*Management of exchange rates within crawling bands:* This is the pegging but with margin higher than target zone. This arrangement is used for transition from pegging to floating exchange rate.

*Managed floating exchange rates:* In this arrangement countries manage their exchange rate with foreign currency (or a basket of currencies) within a wide margin. These countries have their monetary policy and manipulate exchange rate for favorable balance of payment and other indicators like inflation and unemployment. Tanzania, Uruguay, Ukraine use this arrangement.

*Free/Independent floating exchange rate:* In this arrangement countries do not intervene in determining the exchange rate. Exchange rate is determined by the market forces. Countries with this arrangement only intervene to reduce short term fluctuations. Australia, Canada and Japan are some examples for independent or free floating exchange rate.

Effects of exchange rates on countries' international trade and capital flows

When exchange rate changes it affects the quantity and bill of imports. If domestic currency depreciates the goods from other country becomes dearer for domestic residents because they need more domestic currency to buy foreign goods now. As a result imports decreases with currency depreciation. On the other hand if domestic currency appreciates the imports increases.

When domestic currency depreciates the domestic goods become cheaper for the foreigners. So in case of currency depreciations the exports increase and vice versa.

Countries (mostly developing) use this currency depreciation method to decrease the deficit in balance of payment.

When currency depreciates the foreigner investors are attracted as now they need fewer funds to invest. On the other hand appreciation in domestic currency makes somewhat less attraction for the foreign investor.

**Elasticity approach:** This approach suggests that depreciation in domestic currency only makes balance of payment favorable if the elasticities of imports and exports are greater than one. Elasticity of imports and exports is greater than one if the imports are luxury goods, have more proportion in the expenses and have close substitutes.

**J curve** suggests that the depreciation will not affect the balance of payment in short run as the payments of import and export goods are normally made in future. But as the time passes the effect of changes in exchange rate start to show its affect. Elasticity approach does not consider capital flow with changes in exchange rate (a drawback of this approach).

**Absorption approach:** It suggests that when economy is operating less than full employment and currency depreciates the domestic goods/services and assets becomes more attractive and foreign goods/services and assets become less attractive. As a result domestic income and expenditures increases and expenditures on foreign goods/services decrease. Foreigners purchase more domestic assets. Increase in income is more than expenditures. So the balance of payment improves by foreign investment and less imports.

On the other hand if the economy is operating at full employment level (optimal capacity) and currency depreciates the aggregate supply cannot be increased while domestic demand will increase.

As a result the price level will increase the imports and exports will go back to its original level (trade deficit), foreign investor will not be attractive to domestic goods/services and it will reverse the effect of currency depreciation on balance of payment.

That's all for the economics. I hope you have enjoyed it. More books are coming in this series. Please review this book as you all did for financial reporting and analysis. Your reviews and suggestions matter a lot to me.

## 3: Describe common objectives of capital restrictions imposed by governments.

Governments impose restrictions on inflow and outflow of capital to attain following objectives.

1. **Support domestic investment:** Especially underdeveloped and developing countries need to have stable capital accumulation growth by using domestic savings. Foreign investment is considered to be more volatile and can go away in hard times. So countries impose restrictions on foreign investments.

2. **To protect domestic producers:** Foreign companies are usually more competitive than domestic companies (if domestic companies are also competitive there is no need of restrictions). Governments impose these restrictions to save the domestic producers from getting out of the market.

3. **National security:** Government restricts foreign investment in some strategic areas to secure the country. For example local oil importer or producer is more desirable than foreigner for military to get oil in case of emergencies like war.

4. **Government revenues:** Governments imposes tariffs on foreign investments and capital movements to generate

revenues.

**5.** A haphazard outflow can also create a lot of problems for the domestic country. Government can also reduce these outflows by imposing restrictions.

# LEARNING MODULE 8

## EXCHANGE RATE CALCULATION

**1: Calculate and interpret currency cross-rates.**

We can calculate the exchange rate of a currency by using division and multiplication of other exchange rate. This is called currency cross rate of resulting currency. Currency cross rate are used to calculate exchange rate when there is no active foreign exchange market for that currency is available.

For example if we have a quotation of USD/Euro and Euro/CAD then we can calculate USD/CAD as follows;

USD/CAD = USD/Euro x Euro/CAD.

Let's solve with the help of an example.

USD/Euro = 1.15      Euro/CAD = 2
USD/CAD = USD/Euro x Euro/CAD = 1.15 x 2 = 2.3
It means USD/CAD is 2.3. The cross rate 2.3USD per one CAD.
We can invert the USD/CAD to get CAD/USD quotation like 1/ USD/CAD = 1/2.3 = 0.4347

We can also divide two currencies to get desired results.

**2: Explain the arbitrage relationship between spot rates, forward rates, and interest rates calculate a forward rate using points or in percentage terms, and interpret a forward discount or premium**

### Arbitrage relationship between spot rates, forward rates, and interest rates

In freely traded spot and forward currencies contracts, the

percentage differences between forward and spot rates are almost equal to the differences between interest rates of two currencies. This is possible due to the existence of arbitrage trades.

An investor has two options to invest

- Invest at domestic risk free rate
- Invest at foreign risk free rate

If the investor chooses to invest domestically she needs domestic currency and at end of the period she will have (1+ id). If she chooses to invest in foreign market she need to convert domestic currency with foreign currency at spot rate and earn (1+if) and then convert is at forward rate to get revenues in domestic currency.

The relationship between these three can be expressed with the help of following formula.

Forward rate = spot rate x $\{(1 + if)/(1 + id)\}$

## Calculation and interpretation of a forward discount or premium

If the spot rate is greater than forward rate the situation is called **forward discount**. It means the currency will depreciate in coming days. For example if USD/Euro spot is 1.15USD and 3-month forward is trading at 1.10$ the USD is going to appreciate while Euro is going to be depreciated as we are moving to the maturity of forward contract. We will need less USD to buy one Euro.

The Forward premium is opposite to the forward discount. When Spot rate is less than forward rate the situation is called forward premium. For example Spot rate for USD/Euro is 1.15 and 3-month forward rate is 1.20$. This is called forward premium. We will need more dollars to buy one Euro.

The currency with higher (lower) interest rate will be traded at discount (premium) in forward market.

### Calculation of discount/premium
Spot rate for USD/Euro is 1.15 and 6-month forward rate is 1.20$.

Calculate forward discount/premium.

Forward discount/premium on euro (we calculate this with respect to the denominator currency) = $\frac{\text{Forward rate}}{\text{Spot rate}} - 1$

$= \frac{1.20}{1.15} - 1 = 4.347\%$

This is positive so it is at premium. This is interpreted as the premium on the Euro in forward market is 4.347%.

We can annualize this premium. Since this forward contract is of 6-month so by multiplying by two we can have annualized premium.

## Calculation of a forward rate

Forward exchange rates are different from spot rates. Forward rates are quoted as difference between spot and forward rates. There are many ways in which forward rates can be expressed and point base is one of them. These points are added or subtracted from the spot rate to get forward rates. When these points are added (subtracted) to spot rate this is called forward premium (discount). The unit of point is the last decimal place in the spot quote rate.

*Example*

*The USD/Euro spot rate is 1.15USD with 6-month forward rate quoted at +2.4 points. What is the USD/Euro 6-month forward rate?*

The spot rate is 1.15 so each point of forward rate is 1/100 th . So the forward rate is 1.15 + 0.024 = 1.174. (The forward rate is 0.024 more than spot rate). If the forward rate is negative we would subtracted it.

When the forward rate is given in percentage we simply subtract the percentage from 1 and multiply the result with spot rate.

*Example:*

*Spot rate for USD/Euro =1.15 and the forward rate is 0.032%. Calculate forward rate.*

*We know 0.032% is 0.00032.*

*Forward rat = 1.15 x (1-0.00032) = 1.1496*

---

www.ingramcontent.com/pod-product-compliance
Lightning Source LLC
Chambersburg PA
CBHW071952210526
45479CB00003B/904